BOOST YOUR
BRAiN
POWER

 ## JOEL LEVY

GW00721742

CICO BOOK
LONDON

First published in 2004 by Cico Books Ltd
32 Great Sutton Street London EC1V 0NB
Copyright © Cico Books 2004

The right of Joel Levy to be identified as author of this text has been asserted by him in accordance with the Copyright, Designs and Patents Act of 1988.

10 9 8 7 6 5 4 3 2 1

A CIP catalogue record for this book is available from the British Library

ISBN 1 903116 74 0

Illustrations:
Rupert Besley
Trina Dalziel
Stephen Dew
Jacqui Mair

Design: David Fordham

PRINTED IN MALAYSIA

CONTENTS

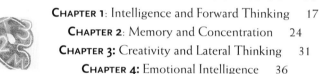

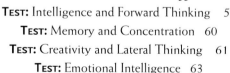

PART I

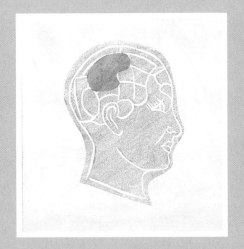

BRAIN BASICS

BRAIN BASICS

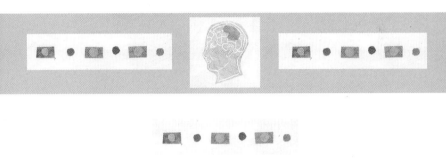

CRADLED INSIDE YOUR SKULL is an unprepossessing lump of pinky-gray tissue, weighing about 3 lb (1.3 kg). It's not much to look at, but this "lump" is the seat of emotion, reason, memory, language, logic, sensation, will, and consciousness. It regulates and directs your body's basic processes, controls your actions, and generates every aspect of your inner life. In this section, we look at the biology that makes this possible, starting with the basic cellular building blocks of the nervous system, and working up to the structure and organization of the brain.

THE NEURON

THE BUILDING BLOCK of the brain and the rest of the nervous system is the nerve cell, or neuron. Your brain contains over 100 billion of these, connected in webs of indescribable complexity (see inset, page 6).

STRUCTURE OF THE NEURON

IN ITS MOST COMMON FORM, a neuron consists of a cell body with many projections leading away from it. Most of these are dendrites, which collect information from other neurons and bring it to the cell body. One of them, much longer than the others, is the axon, which can stretch up to 3 ft (1 m) before branching to make contact with the dendrites of other neurons. In most neurons the axon is coated with a fatty white sheath called myelin, which acts as a kind of insulator, speeding the transmission of nervous signals.

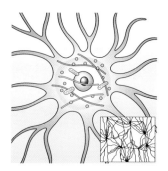

FUNCTION OF THE NEURON

THE NEURON (above) is like a tiny biological microprocessor chip. It collects inputs from other neurons (via the dendrites), processes them (in the cell body), and gives an output (via the axon). The neuron is able to accomplish this because it is electrically charged. By transporting ions across its cell membrane it builds up an electrical potential between the inside and the outside. If the neuron receives enough inputs, a change in the cell membrane is triggered, causing rapid discharge of the electrical potential along its entire length, producing the traveling electrical impulse commonly known as a nervous signal.

Synapses

NERVOUS SIGNALS—the inputs and outputs of neuron function—are transmitted between neurons at a synapse, which is where the axon of one neuron connects to the dendrite of another, separated only by a tiny synaptic gap. When a nerve signal arrives at the end of the axon, small packets of special chemicals, known as neurotransmitters, are released into the gap and are picked up by receptor proteins on the other side (below). If enough signals are picked up, it generates its own electrical impulse and propagates the nervous signal.

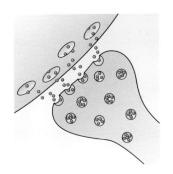

Neurotransmitters

DIFFERENT TRANSMITTERS are used by different types of neurons, or are in different areas of the brain, or they may have differing effects on the same neuron—some will excite the neuron, others will inhibit it, making it less likely to fire. Neurotransmitters play a vital role in controlling brain processes.

By altering the subtle balance of neurotransmitters in the brain, through the use of pharmaceutical or recreational drugs, for instance, it is possible to affect mood, motor control, perception, memory, and even consciousness itself. For example, the neurotransmitter serotonin plays a major role in the production and regulation of emotions and mood. Serotonin levels change over the course of the day and the year, can be affected by the food you eat, and are modified by antidepressants like Prozac and drugs like Ecstasy.

THE CENTRAL NERVOUS SYSTEM

THE BRAIN IS JUST ONE ELEMENT in the nervous system, which can be divided up in many ways. The peripheral nervous system includes the nerves that lead to and from the different parts of your body, including the nerves that signal heat felt on the back of the hand, or that trigger the contraction of your calf muscles. The central nervous system includes the spine, the brain stem, the cerebellum, and the cerebrum.

BASIC DIVISIONS OF THE BRAIN

THE SPINE COMES UP through the base of the skull and swells into the most primitive part of the brain, the brain stem.

● The brain stem controls the unconscious processes of the body, such as breathing, and whether you are awake or asleep. All nerve signals between the brain and the body and senses, incoming and outgoing, pass through this region, and it is also where nerve signals from the right-hand side of your body cross over to lead to the left-hand side of the brain, and vice versa.

● The cerebellum sits at the base of the brain and controls the complex programs of neuronal firing needed to produce smooth, coordinated, and balanced movement. While you may consciously decide to walk using higher parts of the brain, it is the cerebellum that actually carries out the neural processes involved.

● The cerebrum is what most people mean when they talk about the brain. This is where all your higher mental functions, like thinking, memory, and language, reside, and is also the seat of consciousness. In most other animals, it is much smaller and less developed. The outer surface of the cerebrum, called the cerebral cortex, is deeply wrinkled and fissured so that it looks like a walnut. The extensive wrinkling allows more of it to fit into the skull.

● Between the cerebrum and lower parts of the brain are "in-between" structures that link the conscious processes of the cerebrum to the unconscious processes of the brain stem: the thalamus, hypothalamus, and limbic system. They are involved in generating and regulating the "animal" parts of your personality—your emotions, fears, and basic drives, such as hunger, thirst, and sexual desire. They are also involved in learning and memory formation.

The cerebral hemispheres

THE CEREBRUM itself is divided into two halves, known as the left and right cerebral hemispheres. Although the two hemispheres are anatomically almost identical, they perform different roles. In most people, the left hemisphere is dominant for functions such as language, logic, and mathematical ability, while the right hemisphere is dominant for emotions, art, and spatial reasoning. Each hemisphere controls the sensory and motor functions of the opposite side of the body, but in most people the left hemisphere is dominant for motor control, making them right-handed.

RIGHT- AND LEFT-BRAIN DIFFERENCES

YOU ARE NOT NORMALLY CONSCIOUS of any of this separation of roles, thanks to the corpus callosum, a bridge of neural fibers that connects the two hemispheres, providing a high-speed information transfer link. Messages pass so quickly between the hemispheres that they are able to operate as a single unit.

It is, however, possible to pick up on the difference between the hemispheres by testing your immediate reaction to asymmetrical stimuli. For instance, make an instant decision about which of the faces below looks happier to you.

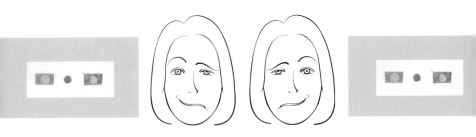

Even though the pictures are simply mirror images of one another, the majority of people pick the right-hand one. Because the right hemisphere is dominant for emotion, it is the information in the left field of vision that has the most immediate impact on your perception of emotion—in this case, it's the right-hand picture, where the smile is to the left of the nose (i.e., in the left field of vision).

ONE-SIDED PEOPLE

OCCASIONALLY, THROUGH stroke, injury, or surgery, one hemisphere of the brain is damaged while the other continues to function. People afflicted in this way can display a condition known as unilateral neglect, where they appear to be unable to perceive or think about one side of space. Symptoms include putting all the numbers in one half when drawing a clock face, as above; eating only half of the food on a plate (if the plate is turned around, the subject is able to eat the other half); and even failing to recognize limbs on the affected side.

LOBES OF THE BRAIN

EACH HEMISPHERE is further divided into four lobes:

● The frontal lobes are at the front of the brain. They deal with the most "intellectual" functions, such as planning, forethought, strategy, will, and self-control. They also contain the main site of voluntary muscle control—the motor cortex—and some language control areas.

● The temporal lobes are on either side of the brain. They are involved in hearing, smell, and making sense of language. Disturbances (such as epilepsy) of this part of the brain are linked to frightening sensations, such as feeling menacing presences, or hearing preternatural sounds.

● The parietal lobes, across the top of the brain, contain the main area of sensory cortex, where sensations from different parts of the body are consciously felt.

● The occipital lobes at the back of the brain are mainly concerned with vision.

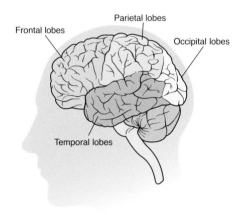

GENDER DIFFERENCES IN THE BRAIN

IT'S WIDELY ASSUMED THAT there are major differences between male and female thinking, and therefore male and female brains. In practice, however, there are very few differences between the two, and even a trained anatomist would be hard put to tell the difference between two brains of different gender but equal size. On the whole, men's brains tend to be bigger and heavier, but this is probably because men tend to be bigger and heavier.

COGNITIVE DIFFERENCES BETWEEN MEN AND WOMEN

NONETHELESS, some differences between male and female minds have been discovered. Women seem to be better, on average, at some verbal tasks and at multitasking (e.g., doing one thing while talking about another) but fare slightly worse than men at some tests of spatial reasoning, such as mentally rotating three-dimensional images. Men are also slightly better, on average, at some tests of navigation/map-reading, which conforms to a popular gender stereotype. It is very important to note, however, that these findings show that the average differences between the sexes are much smaller than the average differences between individuals—in other words, the map-reading abilities of any two men are likely to be just as different as those of a given man and woman.

THE BRAIN THROUGH LIFE

BRAIN DEVELOPMENT begins early in pregnancy—within five weeks of conception the tiny fetus has a proto-spinal cord, which is swollen at the head end where the cerebrum will develop. Between weeks 9 and 12 the fetal brain and nerves start to function, and by week 20, when the fetus is just 7½ in (19 cm) long, it can react to sounds (although this does not mean it has any conscious awareness of them).

Whittling down the brain

RIGHT FROM THE START of pregnancy, the fetal brain cells are speedily replicating and increasing in number. By the time a baby is born, he or she has more neurons than at any point in the rest of his/her life. Over the next few years, many of these cells are "pruned away," to give the brain its fully functional form. Only those cells that are used remain—these get bigger and forge increasing numbers of connections with other cells. The number of support cells, which help to nurture and protect neurons, also grows; an adult has up to 50 times as many support cells as neurons (that's up to 5,000 billion).

Making connections

AS AN INFANT SOAKS UP information about the world and him or herself, billions of new synaptic connections are made. Until around the age of seven, a child's brain is especially pliable and can be rewired on a massive scale. After this age, neurons are rapidly coated with their fatty myelin sheaths, increasing the speed of transmission they can achieve, but limiting their ability to make new connections as quickly. This is what makes childhood such a critical phase for learning. The richer a child's environment and intellectual stimulation, the more connections his or her neurons can make, and the more powerful the brain becomes.

The aging brain

SOME AREAS of the brain undergo additional growth during puberty and the teenage years, but after this, changes happen on a microscopic scale, as the number and pattern of synaptic connections are modified through learning and experience. There are over 100 trillion connections in your brain. Neurons continue to die off, however, and by late adulthood you are losing more than 100,000 nerve cells a day. Compared with the total this is a small proportion, but over the course of your adult life you can expect to lose about 7 percent of your brain cells.

Aging brings gradual changes in the brain—the cortex gets thinner, and fluid-filled spaces called ventricles enlarge slightly. However, neither of these changes actually affects your brain power very much. More serious is the decline in blood supply to the brain, which can slow it down and make it vulnerable to blood clots (causing strokes). The brain also becomes more vulnerable to degenerative diseases such as Alzheimer's, where plaques of protein build up around some neurons, interfering with their function and reducing the density of connections they can make.

REJUVENATING THE BRAIN

THE GOOD NEWS is that there are plenty of things you can do to minimize age-related decline and maximize your mental powers. Exercise and healthy living can maintain blood supply to the brain and protect it against damaging agents, while mental exercise, such as learning, being creative, or undertaking intellectual challenges, can maintain and increase the density of synaptic connections in the brain. The next two sections show you how to achieve this and boost your brain power.

PART II

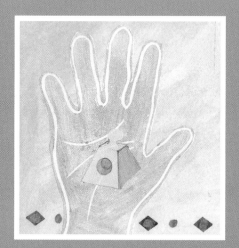

THE MENTAL WORKOUT

CHAPTER 1

INTELLIGENCE AND FORWARD THINKING

INTELLIGENCE IS DEFINED as the ability to learn from experience, acquire knowledge, think abstractly, and adapt to your environment. Intelligence is not the same as knowledge, learning, or ability, though it can improve all three.

HOW DOES INTELLIGENCE WORK?

POPULAR CONCEPTIONS of intelligence are revealed by the phrases people use to describe it—"the ability to figure things out," "how quick or smart you are," "how well you do at school." But when psychologists try to define intelligence they run into trouble, because it quickly becomes obvious that it's a broad concept that covers many different things. One explanation for this is that there are many different types of intelligence.

TYPES OF INTELLIGENCE

DIFFERENT THEORIES describe different types of intelligence. According to one theory there are just two types: crystalized intelligence, which is knowledge that someone has acquired, and fluid intelligence, which is their ability to use this knowledge. According to another theory there are three types of intelligence: abstract intelligence—the ability to work with symbols; concrete intelligence—the ability to work with objects; and social intelligence—the ability to understand and relate to people. Other theories describe anything up to dozens of types; psychologist Robert Steinberg suggests three, while leading theorist Howard Gardner posits seven. Many of these theories, however, are really describing the same things but giving them different names.

SPATIAL, NUMERICAL, AND VERBAL INTELLIGENCE

INTELLIGENCE TESTS typically measure the more abstract aspects of intelligence. If you look at the intelligence test in the Test-Pad, you'll see that the questions are divided up into categories that differ in fairly obvious ways. Some have to do with your ability to think about shapes and mentally manipulate them in space—known as spatial intelligence. Questions that deal with numbers and mathematics test what is known as numerical intelligence.

Other items ask you about words, and involve what is known as verbal intelligence. While verbal intelligence is an important element of intelligence tests, it is also one aspect of a wider area of mental functioning—communication, which includes language and non-verbal communication. This is dealt with in more detail in Chapter 5.

EMOTIONAL INTELLIGENCE

ONE ASPECT OF INTELLIGENCE that used to be neglected, but is now a hot topic of research, is emotional intelligence. This is basically the same as social intelligence, and describes your ability to perceive, understand, and manage your own and other people's emotions, motivations, feelings, and concerns. It is also sometimes described as inter- or intra-personal intelligence. Emotional intelligence is dealt with in more detail in Chapter 4.

BASIC INTELLIGENCE— THE g FACTOR

DIFFERENT PEOPLE PERFORM better in tests of some types of intelligence and worse in others. Your own experience probably backs this up. For instance, you probably know people who are good with numbers but not so good at dealing with people (i.e., they have high numerical intelligence but low emotional intelligence). But is there a common factor that links all the different types of intelligence, and maybe even underlies them all?

Statistical tests on people's scores across all the different types of intelligence tests seem to show that there is a common factor—in other words, that someone who is good at a verbal test is more likely to also be good at a mathematical test. This common factor has been called g, for "general intelligence." g is a measure of someone's raw mental power.

A useful analogy is with race cars. Different cars might have different handling abilities, wheel and tire types, etc., so some cars do better in rallies on stock-car tracks while others perform better on a race track. The different handling characteristics, tire types, and so on are like a person's abilities with different types of problems—e.g., verbal vs. emotional problems.

One factor that will boost the performance of all the cars, whatever their differences, is a more powerful engine. g is the equivalent of engine power. Just as a race car with a more powerful engine is likely to win more races, so a person with a higher level of g is more likely to be successful in their career, academic achievements, and so on.

WHERE IS INTELLIGENCE LOCATED?

BECAUSE THERE IS LITTLE AGREEMENT about exactly what constitutes intelligence, it's hard to say where in the brain it is located. If we think about intelligence as a constellation of different mental functions and abilities, then we can say that it is distributed all over the brain, but primarily in the cortex, the wrinkled outer layer of the brain. More specific abilities can be more precisely located—for instance, the most abstract mental functions, such as logical reasoning and forward planning, are primarily localized in the prefrontal cortex.

The location of g—if it exists at all—is an intriguing mystery. It is unlikely, however, to simply be a property of one part of the brain, and most likely relates to a general feature, such as the speed of transmission of nervous impulses along your neurons, or an innate tendency of your neurons to make connections more or less easily.

WHAT'S YOUR IQ?

INTELLIGENCE IS USUALLY MEASURED with tests that give a score called an Intelligence Quotient (IQ), and are therefore known as IQ tests. When the tests were devised, the scoring system was set so that an IQ of 100 was the average score (see IQ scale below). Although your score on an IQ test is a good indicator of past and future success in life, there are drawbacks to this method of assessing intelligence.

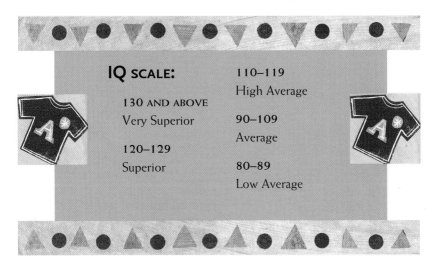

IQ SCALE:

130 AND ABOVE
Very Superior

120–129
Superior

110–119
High Average

90–109
Average

80–89
Low Average

THE IQ CONTROVERSY

FIRST, it has become clear that the tests aren't very good at measuring people's abilities in fine detail—e.g., their common sense, as opposed to their ability to solve abstract problems. Second, IQ tests were designed to help psychologists assess individuals in one-on-one testing as part of a range of tools. All too often, however, the tests are administered to large groups of people, whose scores are used in isolation to categorize them. Third, there is the controversial issue of cultural bias. Although modern tests are designed to avoid this as much as possible, many argue that the tests are inherently biased against some minorities.

IQ testing is associated with many other controversies and questions, from the divisive issue of whether intelligence is genetically and/or racially determined, to the mystery of why average IQ scores seem to have climbed since testing began. IQ testing remains, however, one of the most popular and widely available methods of getting an objective view of your mental abilities.

FORWARD PLANNING

RELATED TO MANY of the components of intelligence discussed above is the ability to forward plan—to assess future challenges, and plan responses and problem-solving strategies accordingly. This is considered to be another of mankind's "highest" mental functions. Forward planning is the mental function involved in everything from chess playing and card games to business planning and deciding where you're going on vacation.

BOOSTING YOUR INTELLIGENCE AND PLANNING ABILITIES

ABILITIES SUCH AS INTELLIGENCE and forward planning are probably the most recently evolved aspects of human psychology, which makes them both fragile and flexible. According to Gamon and Bragdon, in a recent book, "[these] functions are the most malleable and improvable with practice." In other words, giving your highest faculties a workout can help to sharpen them and keep them sharp.

The Test-Pad includes an IQ-style test for you to assess your intelligence before you begin your program of brain-boosting. The 24 questions challenge your verbal, numerical, and spatial reasoning abilities.

CHAPTER 2

MEMORY AND CONCENTRATION

MEMORY CONSISTS OF several different systems that work together to help us form, store, and retrieve information and experiences. The different systems allow us to sort through the flood of information supplied by our senses and select the important stuff to be laid down as memories. In this chapter we'll look at how this process works, and how you can use that knowledge to improve your memory.

MEMORIES IN THE BRAIN

WHAT DO MEMORIES LOOK LIKE? If you could look at the brain under a microscope, would you be able to point to a specific structure that represents a memory? In fact, memories do not exist as simple structures, but as networks. A single memory is composed of a circuit of neurons (nerve cells) that fire in a particular pattern. Anything that sets off one of the neurons in the circuit could trigger that memory, although a different pattern of firing, involving the same circuit of neurons, could trigger a different memory.

TYPES OF MEMORY

ACCORDING TO ONE THEORY, there are three main types of memory—the sensory register, short-term memory (also known as working memory), and long-term memory.

THE SENSORY REGISTER

INFORMATION FROM THE SENSE ORGANS and from other parts of the brain (e.g., your imagination) is held briefly in a very short-term form of memory known as the sensory register. You are not consciously aware of everything held here (there's just too much information to take in at this stage). The mechanism of attention selects information that is important or striking in some way, so that you become consciously aware of it. The rest of the sensory register contents are filtered out and lost before you even knew they were there.

SHORT-TERM MEMORY

THE INFORMATION THAT, for whatever reason, you've focused on, passes to your short-term memory (STM). Information held here is retained for a few seconds only, and unless it is rehearsed (i.e., repeated or thought about some more), it will be lost. STM information can be used immediately, which is why it is sometimes called working memory. Or, if it's sufficiently important or striking, it can be laid down in long-term memory (LTM) through a process known as encoding.

HOW THE BRAIN CREATES MEMORIES

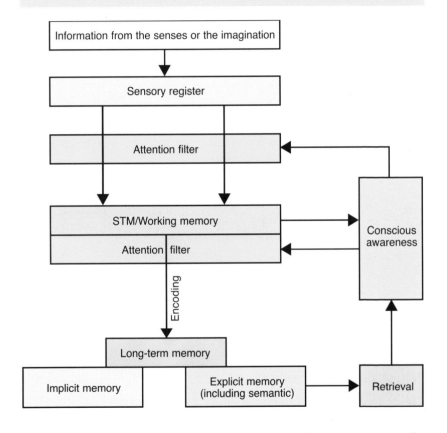

This diagram shows a model of how information, imagination, and experiences are processed in the brain and move between working, short-term, or long-term memory.

One type of information held in working memory is data that comes in discrete packets—good examples are numbers or phonemes (the elements that make up speech). If someone tells you a telephone number that you need to use, the string of digits will be held in your working memory for immediate use. Once you've dialed the number, you no longer have any need to retain the numbers. Your attention switches elsewhere, and you stop rehearsing the numbers, so they are lost—a process known as decay.

There is limited space in your immediate working memory. Most people can store about seven "items"—e.g., seven numbers or seven names. This range is known as your digit-span. If you try to absorb more than this, the new items force out the old ones in a process known as interference.

ENCODING AND RECALL

TO TRANSFER INFORMATION to long-term memory, it must be consciously or unconsciously encoded. The simplest way is rehearsal, but this is not particularly effective—it takes a lot of rehearsal to encode something so that it will last, and so rehearsal is called a shallow encoding method. For more effective encoding, you need to take advantage of the true nature of LTM.

LTMs are not stored as discrete packets of information, but as complex networks of association. For instance, if you remember eating an ice cream, your association network might include the flavor of the ice cream, what the weather was like, what you were looking at when you ate it, where you bought it, etc.

Deep encoding involves drawing connections (either consciously or unconsciously) between new information and other memories or knowledge, to build up a denser web of connections. The more strands in your web, the easier it will be to retrieve the memory in the future, through the process known as recall.

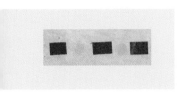

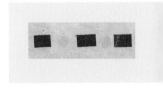

TYPES OF LONG-TERM MEMORIES

NOT ALL LTMs ARE THE SAME. Memories that you can consciously recall are known as explicit memories. Explicit memory includes memory for facts, names, places, etc., which is known as semantic memory. But there is also a type of memory that is not available to your conscious awareness. This is called implicit memory, and includes learned abilities (e.g., riding a bicycle) and things that you don't know you know—for instance, you might think someone looks familiar, but not know why. Your memory of having seen them before is implicit.

IMPROVING YOUR ENCODING

THE KEY TO IMPROVING YOUR MEMORY is to improve the way that you encode information. Memories that are well encoded are longer-lasting, more detailed, and, crucially, easier to recall.

USING YOUR SENSES TO FOCUS ATTENTION

ATTENTION IS WHAT DETERMINES whether you notice and retain information. Events that grab your attention tend to be very memorable. Things that you don't pay proper attention to are likely to be forgotten. You can use your senses to enhance your attentiveness and memory. Make a conscious effort to focus completely on whatever you are doing, taking notice of all the different sensory aspects of the situation. If you are eating a meal, for instance, pay close attention to the tastes, smells, and textures, to the shape and color of the food, and to the sounds around you at the time.

Engaging all of your senses like this will automatically improve your memory, and the more you practice it, the more naturally it will come.

VISUALIZATION AND ASSOCIATION

VISUAL IMAGERY is the most memorable form of information. You can enhance your memory by visualizing things you need to remember. If items do not lend themselves automatically to visualization, associate them with something that does. Association increases the number of connections between memories and makes them easier to recall. Combining the two methods, by building up combinations of striking imagery and arresting associations, is a great way to maximize your memory powers. The more bizarre and striking the imagery you use, the better—strange or humorous juxtapositions are particularly effective.

MNEMONICS

A MNEMONIC IS A memory-enhancing device—a kind of trick to make things such as lists easier to remember. A simple one is to take the first letters of items on a list and use them to make a memorable word or rhyme. The Memory Exercises give more examples of mnemonics.

MUSIC AND MEMORY

R ESEARCH AT THE University of California at Irvine in the 1990s suggested that listening to classical music could enhance the intelligence of children, prompting a flurry of interest and massive sales of Mozart's *Sonata for Two Pianos in D Major*. Subsequent research has more or less debunked the Mozart Effect, but has shown that musical training, rather than simply listening to music, does boost memory power. There is also plenty of anecdotal evidence to suggest that soothing, structured music, like that by Mozart or Bach, can increase concentration levels, which in turn makes for more effective encoding and therefore recall.

CHAPTER 3

CREATIVITY AND LATERAL THINKING

CREATIVITY IS USUALLY DESCRIBED as the ability to make new or unexpected connections between things, a quality that is technically known as divergent thinking or, more familiarly, lateral thinking. For instance, when divergent thinkers solve problems they explore different pathways of thinking, come up with new theories and interpretations, and look at things in unexpected ways.

By contrast, uncreative or convergent thinkers solve problems by following tried and tested paths of thought that they expect to "converge" on the single, correct solution. Once they solve a problem successfully, they expect all similar problems to conform to the same pattern: They are said to have developed a mental set. Mental sets don't just apply to problems—you can develop a mental set about many different types of things, from how you expect people in certain occupations to behave, to how a tool can be used. This may limit your ability to deal with people, things, or ideas creatively.

WHY IS OUR THINKING USUALLY LIMITED?

CONVERGENT THINKING sounds bad, but humans have evolved to think like this for a reason. In a complex world that throws up constant challenges, your success, and sometimes your very survival, depends on dealing with these challenges quickly and effectively. Our minds have evolved to take mental shortcuts so that we can do this.

If you are faced with a large, angry-looking creature that you don't recognize, but which is baring its fangs at you, there's no time to think creatively about what it might be, or how it might behave. You have to fall back on your mental shortcuts—in this case, the mental set that says,"Big, ugly creatures baring their fangs are dangerous, and probably want to eat me: I'd better not stick around!"

Mostly this sort of convergent thinking works well enough, but it can limit your ability to think creatively. In today's world creative thinking is at a premium, so it pays to examine the habits of people who can think this way.

HOW CREATIVE THINKERS WORK

RESEARCH HAS SHOWN that people who are good at thinking creatively don't necessarily have high IQs. Instead, it's three particular personality characteristics that seem to be more important. The first is nonconformity—openness to experience, willingness to take risks or try new things, and lack of concern about conforming to accepted standards.

The second is curiosity. Creative thinkers constantly question, inspect, seek, and probe. This is partly because they are open to novelty (an aspect of nonconformity), but they are also more likely to notice new things, or to spot contradictions or flaws in accepted ways of doing things. When they do notice these, they don't simply accept them, but feel compelled to investigate further.

Finally, although it may sound like a stereotype, creative people display persistence; hence the old adage, often attributed to Albert Einstein, "Genius is ten percent inspiration and ninety percent perspiration." Creative people worry at problems until they find the solution, and may even go further, being unwilling to accept the obvious or conventional solution.

Situational factors (also known as circumstances) also boost creativity. People become more creative when they are in a good mood and are allowed to work without pressure and supervision. Your motivation also makes a difference—if you are motivated to achieve creativity for its own ends, you are more likely to do so than if seeking to serve an ulterior purpose (for instance, making money).

BOOSTING YOUR CREATIVITY AND PROBLEM-SOLVING ABILITIES

LEARNING TO THINK CREATIVELY can make you better at solving problems. The two key principles are learning to think out of the box, and developing a receptive mental state.

THINKING OUT OF THE BOX

CREATIVE THINKING is thinking that makes new or unexpected associations. This is only possible if you can overcome the old and conventional mental sets that usually restrict thinking. A good example of this sort of restrictive mental set is the concept of "functional fixedness." Functional fixedness is where our concept of an object, and how it can be used or what it can be used for, is restricted by the roles and functions most often associated with that object.

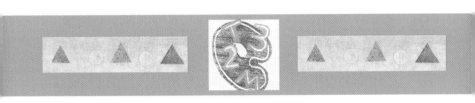

THE CANDLE PROBLEM

A GOOD ILLUSTRATION of this is the Candle Problem, where two groups are challenged to mount a candle on the side of a vertical screen. One group is given a small candle, a box of matches, and a thumbtack. The other group is given the same materials, but with the matches outside of the box. The first group typically struggles with this problem, but the second group much more quickly works out that the solution is to tack the inner tray of the matchbox onto the screen and mount the candle on the matchbox.

The first group struggled because of functional fixedness—because the box contained matches, they could not think of it in any other way than as a container. The second group was able to overcome this because, when the box did not contain the matches, it was easier to think of as a support.

BRAINSTORMING

BRAINSTORMING IS A STRATEGY used to encourage creativity. The idea is that by telling people to come up with any idea, no matter how dumb it sounds, you encourage them to break free of mental sets and think out of the box. Group brainstorming offers the further bonus of feedback, where divergent thinking by one person can be taken further by another.

RECEPTIVE STATE OF MIND

MANY PEOPLE find that the solution to a problem comes to them when they stop trying to think about the problem—in fact, when they are not thinking about anything at all. It's at times such as dropping off to sleep, engaging in an almost automatic task (e.g., driving), or simply winding down at the end of the day, that the most vivid imagery or original ideas can occur. These are precisely the times when the human mind is at its most receptive, because there are no distracting thoughts. Conversely, stress, noise, pressure, and distraction hamper creativity.

Achieving a receptive state of mind means learning to shut off distracting thoughts and outside perceptions, and quiet your physiological as well as mental state. These are the same techniques that are used in meditation and relaxation—see Part III, Chapter 1 for an in-depth discussion.

CHAPTER 4

EMOTIONAL INTELLIGENCE

SOCIAL INTELLIGENCE

As far back as 1920, psychologist E.L. Thorndike described what he called "social intelligence," which he defined as the ability to understand and relate to people. Later, social intelligence was used to explain the evolution of the human brain—according to some theories, humans evolved larger brains as the result of their developing social skills. The more advanced their social abilities became, the more complex human society became, and the greater the need for still better social intelligence, and hence larger brains.

THE IMPORTANCE OF EMOTIONAL INTELLIGENCE

DURING THE 1990S PSYCHOLOGISTS grew to appreciate that social intelligence applied not just to interpersonal interactions (interactions between people) but also to intrapersonal processes (internal mental processes), and coined the term "emotional intelligence" (EI) to cover all aspects of this ability. Research showed that EI plays an important role, not just in relationships but also in the workplace, classroom, and any other sphere where people interact or emotions come into play. On a more personal level, your levels of EI also determine:

- How well you know yourself
- How well you can communicate your needs and feelings
- How well you deal with conflict
- The extent to which you can transform patterns of thinking and behavior so you can grow as a person

People with high levels of EI are more likely to be self-aware, confident, balanced, and fulfilled, and are also better at dealing with other people. They make good salespeople, managers, team workers, and leaders, and also do well in caring professions and other "people jobs."

COMPONENTS OF EI

THERE ARE MANY DIFFERENT WAYS to divide up EI into its component abilities. According to Professor Jack Mayer and Dr. Peter Salovey, the leading researchers and theorizers in the field, it can be divided into five domains:

SELF-AWARENESS: Observing yourself and recognizing feelings as they happen

MANAGING EMOTIONS: Handling feelings so that they are expressed and acted on appropriately; realizing what is behind a feeling; finding ways to cope with fear, anxiety, anger, and sadness

MOTIVATING YOURSELF: Using emotions to help achieve goals; self control; delaying gratification; overcoming damaging impulses

EMPATHY: Sensitivity to other people's feelings and concerns; being able to see things from their perspective; appreciating differences in other people's viewpoints

HANDLING RELATIONSHIPS: Managing emotions in others; social skills; the ability to handle conflict and difficult issues

EQ: MEASURING YOUR EI

To PROVIDE A TOOL for objectively quantifying EI, some psychologists have developed standardized tests that give a rating similar to IQ, which has naturally been dubbed "EQ" (Emotional Quotient). Such tests typically comprise inventories of statements to which you give ratings, multiple-choice-style questions, and visual recognition of emotions in faces. The EQ-Style Test in the Test-Pad combines some of these elements to give you a tool for assessing your own EI.

CAN YOU BOOST YOUR EQ?

As with IQ, psychologists disagree over the extent to which genetics or the environment determines EQ, and therefore how easy it is to improve a low EQ. Even if it is difficult to alter your underlying EI abilities, you can learn to work around a low EI with strategies that improve your emotional "performance." These strategies include making implicit emotional cues more explicit; observing the habits of emotionally intelligent people; and practicing emotional skills.

CHAPTER 5

LANGUAGE AND COMMUNICATION

ONE OF THE HALLMARKS of human intelligence is that it creates its own cultural and social context. It does this through communication, and in particular through the use of language. Language is one of the most complex and advanced cognitive abilities, and yet children too young to use the bathroom or tie their own shoes seem to master it without effort.

But language, in the classic sense of verbal communication, is not the whole story. Nonverbal forms of communication supplement, and sometimes even subvert, spoken words. In this chapter we'll look at both, and show how you can develop your communication skills and keep your mind sharp.

LANGUAGE IN THE BRAIN

LIKE MOST COMPLEX/HIGHER mental functions, language involves many different parts of the brain, depending on the exact task in question—usually several at once. However, three areas are particularly important:

Broca's area

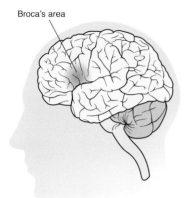

Wernicke's area

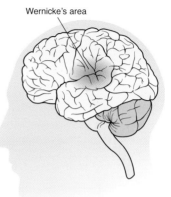

● **BROCA'S AREA:** This is named after the French surgeon who discovered its function in 1861 by studying people who had damage to this part of the brain, and who showed a characteristic dysfunction, now known as Broca's aphasia. It is located on the posterior surface of the left frontal lobe (just about underneath the temple). It controls the production of language and is responsible for fluency and grammar.

● **WERNICKE'S AREA:** Named after a German neurologist, this is located just next to Broca's area, but on the temporal and parietal lobes, nearer the back of the head (just about above the ear). It controls meaning in language and converting sounds into mental concepts, and is responsible for comprehension of spoken and written language.

● **THE INSULA:** This is an area below the surface of the brain, pretty well between Broca's and Wernicke's areas. It controls the actual mechanics of speech, such as pronunciation, timing, and order.

Together, these three areas help us to formulate, understand, and speak language. Other parts of the brain that are important are those that deal with memory—important for remembering meanings, spelling and some grammar, and word forms; the senses—especially hearing for speech and vision for body language and writing; and motor skills—for operating the vocal cords, tongue, and mouth.

How language develops

CHILDREN PICK UP LANGUAGE in the natural course of their development, and they seem to do it in much the same way around the world, no matter what language they are learning. Although they are obviously not born able to write and speak, they are equipped with a built-in language-acquisition device. This is an innate ability to absorb language from parents and other adults, and to automatically develop vocabulary, grammar, and all the other elements that make someone a fluent speaker.

Stages in language formation

FROM AROUND the age of four to six months infants start to make vocalizations such as coos, grunts, and sounds similar to vowels and consonants. From six months to about a year, infants reach the babbling stage. Babies from all over the world, and even deaf babies, seem to babble in the same way, suggesting that the tendency to do so is hardwired into the child. After about a year children start to form actual words and by age three they progress to clauses, reaching properly grammatical speech at around age four.

The progress and degree of development of each stage depends on interaction with caregivers. Children learn by repeating sounds and words made by adults, and from the feedback that adults give to them. The more parents communicate with children, the more language they pick up.

THE CRITICAL WINDOW

THE AUTOMATIC LANGUAGE-ACQUISITION device seems to stay in operation until around the age of 12, over a period known as the critical window for language development. After puberty, this ability is lost, possibly because the neurons in the post-pubertal brain aren't able to make new connections so quickly. This is why it is much easier for children to pick up languages than adults. After this age, learning new languages seems to involve different parts of the brain from the parts that deal with genuinely fluent use of language, so a late learner may never become truly fluent.

NONVERBAL COMMUNICATION

EVEN BEFORE THEY START TO DEVELOP their verbal skills, infants can respond to and initiate nonverbal forms of communication, such as smiling, eye widening, nose wrinkling, following others' glances, and pointing fingers. Debate rages over whether expressions such as smiles, frowns, and nose wrinkles (to display disgust) are learned or innate, but they are universal across human cultures, so that your answers to the expression-matching test in Chapter 4 (Emotional Intelligence) would be the same as those of a Xhosa bushman or a New Guinea forest dweller.

BODY LANGUAGE

FACIAL EXPRESSIONS are perhaps the most obvious form of nonverbal communication. A more subtle form is body language. The way that you stand, sit, or lean, what you do with your arms, legs, hands, and feet, where you look, when and how often you move, and how you do all of these things in relation to other people—these are all means of communicating, or ways of passing on information about your mental and emotional state, motivations, and reservations. Some of the main categories of meaning signaled by body language are dominance/submission, attraction/dislike, agreement/disagreement, sincerity/insincerity, and interest/boredom.

Often you are not fully aware of either sending or receiving messages in this way, but you can easily become more aware, and so improve your communication skills. The Body Language Vocabulary Cards depict some of the main "words" or "phrases" used in body language.

IMPROVING YOUR LANGUAGE ABILITIES

JUST BECAUSE YOUR BRAIN has lost its natural ability to learn simply by listening doesn't mean that learning new languages and developing your existing language abilities can't help your brain. Some research suggests that learning helps to maintain neurons in the state where they can still make many new connections, effectively keeping your brain young. Such "mental workouts" may be able to stave off age-related cognitive decline, and even Alzheimer's disease.

Three strategies for maintaining and improving your language abilities are:

● **READING:** Increases vocabulary and exposes you to challenging grammatical forms. The more advanced or difficult the reading matter, the better.

● **WORD GAMES:** Crosswords, acrostics (where the initial letters of words or lines in a piece make up a word themselves, and so on can all help with verbal abilities, as well as stimulating memory, problem solving, and creative thinking abilities.

● **LEARNING A LANGUAGE:** This stimulates most parts of the intellect and has practical and social advantages, too.

IMPROVING YOUR NONVERBAL COMMUNICATION SKILLS

ALTHOUGH MOST OF US use body language in instinctive fashion, without being aware of it, you can train yourself to make better use of it, and to read other people's nonverbal messages more successfully. The first step is to develop awareness. Observing yourself in the mirror, or, even better, on videotape, can provide surprising feedback on how you present yourself to others, in the same way that hearing your own voice on audiotape is often a shock. Making a habit of people-watching when you're out and about is a good way to become more aware of other people's body language. The Body Language Challenge cards give you specific guidelines on how to do this and what to look out for.

PART III

YOUR MENTAL HEALTH

CHAPTER 1

SLEEPING AND RELAXATION

SLEEPING IS UNIVERSAL above a certain level of complexity in the animal kingdom. Worms do not sleep, but even fish have "rest," periods of lowered physiological and neural activity. Humans spend around a third of their lives sleeping. Sleep deprivation is distressing and rapidly fatal—after 60 hours you would experience significant mental deficits, after around four days hallucinations, and eventually death.

THE FUNCTION OF SLEEP

EVIDENTLY SLEEP IS IMPORTANT, yet we still do not know exactly what it is for. Several different functions have been suggested, which may all be true to varying extents. The main purposes of sleep are thought to be:

● **BODILY RESTORATION:** Sleep restores bodily energy levels and allows restorative processes time to work.

● **MENTAL RESTORATION:** Sleep is necessary for maintenance of mental energy levels.

● **LEARNING AND MEMORY:** Sleep is when information absorbed during the day is consolidated, and some of the total information is jettisoned in a kind of mental housekeeping.

THE STRUCTURE OF SLEEP

BY OBSERVING SLEEPERS in laboratory conditions and recording their brain activity, eye movements, muscle tension, and breathing, psychologists have discovered that there are different kinds of sleep and that a typical night's sleep follows a characteristic pattern.

ORDINARY SLEEP

WHEN YOU FIRST DROP OFF to sleep, you enter Stage 1 of what is called non-rapid eye movement (NREM) sleep. This stage is light sleep, from which you are easily woken. After around seven minutes you drop into Stage 2 sleep, and over the next 10–25 minutes you fall into Stage 3, and then Stage 4, or deep sleep. During Stage 4 sleep, most brain activity slows right down, and only the brain stem—the part of the brain that controls basic functions, such as breathing—continues to operate normally.

REM SLEEP

AFTER A PERIOD OF DEEP SLEEP, your brain stem sends out arousal signals and prods your cerebral cortex back into consciousness, albeit a special form of consciousness. You are now entering the fifth phase of sleep—rapid eye movement (REM) sleep, when dreams take place.

During REM sleep, your conscious mind is cut off from your senses and your muscles (except for the eye muscles), so that you cannot act out your dreams. Sometimes this protective mechanism fails, and the result is sleeptalking, or even sleepwalking. Even in normal sleep some level of your consciousness remains wired up to the outside world—for example, if a telephone rings, the sound may be incorporated into your dream.

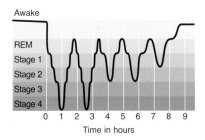

THE SLEEP CYCLE

AN ADULT GENERALLY PASSES THROUGH the five phases of sleep roughly every 90 minutes (above), although the time spent in each phase changes over the course of the night, and over the course of a life. When you first drop off, you spend more time in deep sleep and only a couple of minutes in REM sleep, but by the next morning your REM phases may be up to 30 minutes long.

HEALTHY SLEEP HABITS

MEN NEED, ON AVERAGE, eight hours' sleep a night to feel properly rested, while women need seven. If you get less than this, you start to suffer side effects during waking hours—impaired concentration and memory, learning difficulties, mental slowness, impaired reactions, co-ordination, and movement, and, of course, fatigue.

Contrary to popular belief, however, you cannot simply make up sleep deficits by sleeping longer weekends. In fact, sleeping late can disrupt your normal sleeping habits, making things worse. Here are a few healthy sleeping habits you should practice:

- Try to get your recommended daily amount of sleep.
- Go to bed when you feel tired.
- Prepare for sleep by avoiding eating or overstimulating activities, like watching TV, just beforehand.
- Keep TVs, computers, work, and so on out of your bedroom. Bedrooms should be used only for sleeping and sex.
- Stick to a regular sleep routine, including at weekends.
- Avoid alcohol, cigarettes, and caffeine for at least four hours before bedtime— they interfere with healthy sleeping patterns so that you don't get the full benefit.
- People with chronic snoring should consult a physician or sleep specialist to make sure they are not suffering from sleep apnea, a condition that interferes with healthy sleeping patterns and can cause fatigue.
- Practice relaxation techniques to help prevent stress-related insomnia.

DREAMS

YOU CAN HAVE DREAMS during both non-REM sleep and REM sleep, but the latter are the ones you are most likely to remember. They tend to be more vivid, more likely to have a narrative, and more likely to involve emotive, strange, or unsettling events and scenarios. Most people dream about five times during each eight-hour period of sleep, meaning that you have about 1,825 dreams each year.

WHAT ARE DREAMS FOR?

THE PURPOSE AND MEANING OF DREAMS, if any, has attracted the interest of philosophers and artists throughout history. There are three main theories:

● Dreams are the imaginary acting out of repressed and unconscious desires, represented symbolically. This theory was first proposed by Freud, and developed much further by Jung, who theorized that during dreams we encounter archetypes—symbols that are common to every subconscious mind. In interacting with these archetypes, we are encountering forces of nature. Both Freud and Jung saw dreams as a great opportunity for insight into the psyche.

● Dreams represent conscious concerns, fears, hopes, and anxieties, but transformed into different images. This theory is related to Freud's but is a lot more straightforward. Again, the implication is that by exploring your dreams you can learn about your psyche.

● Dreams are a way of going over information gathered during the day, filtering out junk, selecting and rehearsing the important stuff, and integrating it with instincts and knowledge already present. Dreams are essential for learning, especially for the developing mind of an infant, which might explain why newborn babies spend up to 70 percent of their sleep time in REM sleep.

CAN DREAMS HELP YOU?

APART FROM OFFERING POTENTIAL INSIGHTS into your conscious and subconscious mind, there is also the intriguing possibility that dreams provide a forum for enhanced creativity. Several prominent scientists report stories of how they struggled with a seemingly intractable problem, only to dream the solution. The story of Kekule, discoverer of the structure of benzene (at the time a difficult question in chemistry), is a classic example. He nodded off pondering on the problem, and dreamed of a snake swallowing its own tail. On awaking, the circular image led him to realize that a ring structure explained the strange chemistry of benzene.

The dream world is a place where many of the rules of creativity (see Part II, Chapter 3) apply. Perhaps, therefore, it's the best place to find creative solutions to problems, if you can prime your sleeping mind to dream about them (see the card on Dream Incubation).

RELAXATION AND THE BRAIN

SLEEP IS NOT THE ONLY restorative process available to you. Everybody needs rest time during waking hours in order to recharge batteries. Crucially, this does not mean a period simply of physical inactivity, but of mental respite. In the modern world, such a respite is increasingly rare, as time is filled with work, travel, or watching television. (Many people talk of "relaxing in front of the TV," but this is one of the great misconceptions of modern life—watching TV is a form of mental stimulation, not relaxation.)

THE BENEFITS OF RELAXATION

MAKING TIME TO PRACTICE relaxation techniques can produce physiological, psychological, and emotional benefits. High blood pressure and cardiovascular problems have both been linked to stress. Relaxation can help to prevent, lower, or improve both. It also helps prevent irritability and mood swings, aids concentration, memory, and learning, and can even help with mental illness. Use the relaxation cards to guide your program. Start with the breathing exercises on the cards, as this skill is central to effective relaxation.

Chapter 2

NUTRITION AND LIFESTYLE

ALL THE MENTAL TRAINING AND HONING in the world won't do you much good if you don't make sure your brain gets the nutrients it needs, while protecting it from the slings and arrows of outrageous lifestyle habits. Diet and lifestyle lay the foundations for optimum brain health, and therefore optimum mental functioning. Unless you give yourself the right dietary and lifestyle platform, you won't be able to make the most of your intellectual gifts.

FEED YOUR MIND

WE OFTEN HEAR TALK of brain food, but what does this really mean? Your brain needs all the same food groups as the rest of your body, but there are some particular nutrients and foodstuffs that are necessary for optimal brain health, and in which the average diet is deficient. This section outlines the main types of nutrient that you need. To learn where to find them, see the Macronutrient and Micronutrient Challenge cards.

THE MAIN FOOD GROUPS

THE MAIN THREE TYPES of macronutrients are protein, carbohydrate, and fat.

● **PROTEIN:** The diets of most people in the Western world include an excess of protein, but even so, we often risk missing out on some vital ones. Proteins are made up of subunits called amino acids, which come in 20 different varieties. Your body can synthesize most of these for itself, but there are eight that must be obtained from your diet. The best way to ensure that you get all of these is to eat a variety of protein foods—this is particularly important for vegetarians.

● **CARBOHYDRATE:** The brain accounts for just 2 percent of your body weight, but uses up 30 percent of your daily calorie intake! It's an energy-hungry organ that needs constant fueling, so skipping meals can result in impaired mental function. This is especially true of breakfast, when your brain needs fresh energy sources to help it tool up for the day, yet unfortunately this is the most commonly missed meal. Research shows that for both children and adults, missing breakfast impairs concentration, learning, and memory, and makes you unhappy, irritable, and lethargic.

Most of the fuel you need is provided by carbohydrates, but all carbohydrates are not the same. Simple carbohydrates, which you find in processed and refined foods (e.g., white bread, junk food, cakes, candy, sugar, etc.), raise your blood sugar levels too fast, and can actually damage your health. Complex carbohydrates are much better, releasing sugar into your bloodstream slowly and steadily, and maintaining the optimal supply of fuel to your brain.

Breakfast is the ideal time to load up on complex carbohydrates. However, the same foods can cause drowsiness if eaten at lunchtime, so make your lunches protein-rich and low in carbohydrates and fat.

● **FAT:** Not all fat is bad, and the brain is particularly hungry for a type of fat called essential fatty acids (EFAs)—in fact, most people don't get enough of these. So while you should seek to lower your intake of saturated fat (found in oils that have been heated, such as those used for frying, fried foods, red meat, junk food, butter, cheese, cakes, potato chips, etc.), you almost certainly need to increase your EFA intake.

BRAIN-BOOSTING MICRONUTRIENTS

MICRONUTRIENTS ARE NUTRIENTS that are essential to health but are only required in minute quantities. Nevertheless, some doctors and nutritionists believe that almost everybody is slightly deficient in many of the key micronutrients. Important micronutrients include:

● **VITAMIN B12:** Needed for the outsides of nerve cells. Deficiency can lead to numbness and tingling in the limbs. High levels may help to prevent age-related cognitive decline. Older people are particularly at risk of deficiency, because they make fewer of the proteins that help with B12 uptake and often have poor diets.

● **MAGNESIUM:** Needed for memory formation and emotional regulation.

● **IRON:** Needed for oxygen transfer to brain cells. Deficiency can cause fatigue and poor concentration. High intake can improve concentration and learning.

● **FOLIC ACID (OR FOLATE):** Deficiency can cause fetal developmental disorders and, in adults, impaired cognitive function, depression, and dementia.

● **CALCIUM:** Needed for nerve signaling. Deficiency can cause muscle twitching and fatigue.

● **POTASSIUM:** Also involved in nerve signaling. Deficiency can cause apathy and weakness.

LIFESTYLE AND THE BRAIN

DIET IS JUST ONE ASPECT of your lifestyle, which incorporates everything about how you live, what you do to your body, and what you put into it. Factors that adversely affect your mental abilities are those that impair your brain's health by reducing the supply of blood, oxygen, and nutrients, exposing it to toxins, and not giving it sufficient time and materials for self-maintenance and repair. Lifestyle factors that enhance your mental functioning are those that boost blood supply to the brain, reduce its exposure to toxins, and give it the time and materials to look after itself.

ADVERSE LIFESTYLE FACTORS

● **SMOKING:** This harms your brain in a variety of direct and indirect ways. It directly reduces the amount of oxygen reaching the brain and increases its exposure to cancer-causing agents. It impairs circulation, indirectly reducing the blood supply to the brain. Nicotine also interrupts healthy sleep patterns.

Quitting smoking is hard, because smoking is a physiological and psychological addiction. Most smokers are aware of the health risks, but one problem is that these risks are not immediate, so it is easy to ignore them for the present. Use the Why I'm Going To Quit Smoking card to provide instantly accessible motivation for quitting.

● **ALCOHOL:** This is OK in very moderate quantities, but large amounts can directly damage the brain, causing large holes to open up. It also directly affects many brain processes (causing intoxication).

● **DRUGS:** In many cases, long-term use of drugs has been linked to impaired memory, poor concentration, and an increased risk of psychiatric problems, from anxiety and paranoia through depression and schizophrenia.

● **LATE NIGHTS:** As explained in the last chapter, sleep is important for mental and physical regeneration and recharging.

● **CAFFEINE:** This raises stress levels, causes nervous tension, and reduces the ability to relax. It interferes with sleep and is addictive, causing mild withdrawal symptoms when missed.

POSITIVE LIFESTYLE FACTORS

● **EXERCISE:** This boosts brain health by improving circulation and lung capacity, and therefore the supply of oxygen and nutrients to the brain. It improves mood, and has been shown to be as effective against depression as antidepressants.

● **RELAXATION SKILLS:** See previous chapter.

SELF-TESTS: SOLUTIONS

The scores and assessments for all the self-tests in the Test-Pad are given in this section.

HOW ARE YOU WIRED?

SCORING

Q	a	b	c	Q	a	b	c	Q	a	b	c
1	3	1	2	9	3	1	2	17	2	3	1
2	1	2	3	10	1	2	3	18	2	1	3
3	3	1	2	11	1	2	3	19	1	2	3
4	2	3	1	12	2	1	3	20	3	1	2
5	3	2	1	13	3	2	1	21	1	1	3
6	3	1	2	14	2	3	1	22	1	3	2
7	3	2	1	15	3	2	1	23	1	1	3
8	1	2	3	16	3	2	1				

HOW DID YOU SCORE?

23–36: You have a low opinion of your mental abilities and may also be lacking vital knowledge about how to look after your brain and maintain its capacity. Maybe some aspects are letting you down more than others—work on these, and you can boost both your mental powers and your self-esteem.

37–56: You share similar overall levels of ability with the vast majority of your family members, friends, and colleagues, but your individual mental makeup has its own unique pattern, with strengths on which you can build and weaknesses you need to tackle.

57–69: You have a high opinion of your own mental abilities, and are well informed about how to get the most out of your brain. See page 1 of the Test-Pad for a more precise picture—you may find room for improvement .

INTELLIGENCE AND FORWARD THINKING

ANSWERS TO IQ-STYLE TEST: SCORE 1 POINT FOR EACH CORRECT ANSWER

1: b; 2: d; 3: b; 4: c; 5: c; 6: a; 7: c; 8: a; 9: d; 10: d; 11: c; 12: d; 13: b;14: b; 15: centre, 2nd row, 16: 5.

HOW DID YOU SCORE?

5 OR LESS: BELOW AVERAGE ● **6–11:** AVERAGE ● **12–14:** ABOVE AVERAGE ● **15–16:** GIFTED

Break down your score into the three different abilities tested here. Questions 1–7 test your verbal reasoning ability; questions 8–14 test your numerical reasoning ability; questions 15–16 test your spatial reasoning ability. Did you get fewer than half the questions right in any of these categories?

If so, this could be an area on which you need to work. Don't take your result too seriously—this is not a standardized intelligence test and cannot be used to accurately ascertain your IQ. For that, you'll need a full-length IQ test, such as the Stanford-Binet Scale or Wechsler Adult-Intelligence Scale, with dozens of items that need to be done under timed conditions.

MEMORY AND CONCENTRATION

ANSWERS TO GENERAL KNOWLEDGE QUIZ

1: Mercury, Venus, Earth, Mars, Jupiter, Saturn, Uranus, Neptune, Pluto (**1 point each**)

2: WORLD WAR I: July 1914–November 1918; WORLD WAR II: September 1939–May 1945 (VE Day)/August 1945 (VJ Day) (**1 point for each of the five dates**)

3: CONTINENTS: Africa, North America, South America, Europe, Asia, Australia, Antarctica. Oceans: Pacific, Atlantic, Indian, Arctic (**Southern is optional—don't score for this; 1 point each for others**)

4: COMEDIES ARE: All's Well That Ends Well; As You Like It; The Comedy of Errors; Cymbeline; Love's Labours Lost; Measure for Measure; The Merry Wives of Windsor; The Merchant of Venice; A Midsummer Night's Dream; Much Ado About Nothing; Pericles; The Taming of the Shrew; The Tempest; Troilus and Cressida; Twelfth Night; Two Gentlemen of Verona; The Winter's Tale. HISTORIES ARE: Henry IV, part 1; Henry IV, part 2; Henry V; Henry VI, part 1; Henry VI, part 2; Henry VI, part 3; Henry VIII; King John; Richard II; Richard III. TRAGEDIES ARE: Antony and Cleopatra; Coriolanus; Hamlet; Julius Caesar; King Lear; Macbeth; Othello; Romeo and Juliet; Timon of Athens; Titus Andronicus. (**1 point for each**)

5: Oslo, Stockholm, Bern, Ottawa, Santiago, Lima, Pretoria, Cairo, Nairobi, Canberra, Kuala Lumpur, Islamabad, Tehran, Kiev (**1 point each**)

6: Nile, Amazon, Yangtze (Chang Jiang), Mississippi–Missouri (**1 point for Nile, Amazon, and Mississippi–Missouri, 2 for Yangtze**)

7: I wandered lonely as a cloud
That floats on high o'er vales and hills,
When all at once I saw a crowd,
A host, of golden daffodils (**1 point for each line**)

8: The sum of the squares of the other two sides (**1 point**)

9a): Boyle's Law (**2 points**)   b): Hooke's Law (**2 points**)

HOW DID YOU SCORE?

LESS THAN 28: Your long-term semantic memory is creaky, either through lack of original encoding (i.e., you weren't paying attention in class) or through poor recall. Improve both your encoding and your powers of recall through practice, and through using the methods outlined in the Exercises on the cards.

29–51: Not bad, but there's room for improvement. Again, use the Exercises to improve your encoding and recall.

52 OR MORE: You have good long-term semantic memory, which suggests that you are skilled at both encoding and recall. Even if you didn't miss any of the answers, you probably struggled with a few of them, so consider using the Exercises to boost your memory powers even more.

SHORT-TERM MEMORY QUIZ

1a: 1 point b: 1 point c: 1 point
2a: 1 point b: 1 point c: 2 points
3: If Yes, score 1 point
4a: 1 point if both b: 1 point for each c: 1 point for name, 2 for number d: 1 point for name, 2 for number e: 1 point for name, 3 for number
5a: 1 point if both b: 1 point for each c: 1 point for name, 2 for number d: 1 point for name, 2 for number e: 1 point for name, 3 for number
6: 1 point for theme, 3 for product

HOW DID YOU SCORE?

0–10: You have a terrible short-term memory! But don't worry, this book can help—practice the Exercises diligently and you can learn the tricks and tactics to boost your short-term memory powers.

11–25: Isn't it surprising how quickly you forget everyday things? Use the Exercises to change the way you pay attention to events and retain everyday information.

26 or more: Your short-term memory is good, which probably indicates that you make full use of your senses to maximize your awareness of everyday events, helping you to recall them at short notice. Even if you didn't miss any of the answers, you probably struggled with a few of them, so use the Exercises to boost your memory powers.

CREATIVITY AND LATERAL THINKING

CREATIVE PROBLEM-SOLVING TEST

Score 1 point for each correct answer.

1: THE REMOTE ASSOCIATES TEST

Answers: **a:** back; **b:** party; **c:** book; **d:** play; **e:** paper; **f:** match; **g:** cheese; **h:** quick.

2: THE FOX, CORN, AND CHICKEN PUZZLE

SOLUTION

You have to take the chicken across, leave her on the far bank, and then come back and pick up the fox and ferry him across. You are now on the far bank with the fox and the chicken. Next, crucially, you take the chicken back with you to the near bank, swap her for the corn, leave the corn with the fox on the far bank, and come back to pick up the chicken.

COMMENT

To solve this problem, you have to make the conceptual leap to realizing that you can carry items both ways! Because of the way the problem is stated, it doesn't occur to most people that this is possible—it requires either a flash of lateral thinking, or a lot of head-scratching until the answer is stumbled upon by accident.

3: THE BUS DRIVER RIDDLE

SOLUTION

The bus driver's name is your name! You were told at the start to "imagine that you are a bus driver."

COMMENT

Most people dismiss this as a dumb joke that cannot be answered because they focus on the wrong information. They assume, while reading the riddle, that it must conform to the usual pattern for numerical/mathematical riddles (i.e., they assume that you have to do mental arithmetic to keep track of who is on the bus). The nonconformist or creative thinker is able to overcome misleading assumptions like this, and find his or her way to a solution by focusing only on the critical elements of a problem.

4: THE NINE DOT PROBLEM

COMMENT

Many people have trouble with this one because they can't break free of the mind-set that views the nine dots as a square. The concept of a square has functional fixedness, carrying with it the assumption that you can't extend your lines beyond the "boundaries" of the square. Only by breaking free of this mind-set, and literally thinking outside the box, can you find the solution.

SOLUTION

5: THE MESSENGER'S PROBLEM

SOLUTION

Use two support trucks in addition to your own. All three of you set off for one day's drive, using up a can of fuel each, at the end of which the first truck transfers one can of fuel to you and one can to the remaining support truck, so that both of you are once again carrying the maximum number of fuel cans. The first truck then has enough fuel to drive one day back to home base. You and the other truck carry on for another day, again using up a can of fuel each. At the end of the day the second truck transfers one can of fuel to you, leaving him with two cans (enough to get back to base) and you with a full load of four cans—enough to get to the other base and deliver your message.

COMMENT

The conceptual hurdle that you have to overcome to solve this problem is to realize that the support trucks have to accompany you only part of the way, and don't have to travel the same distance as each other. The creative thinker realizes there is no rule that says all the trucks need to go all the way.

HOW DID YOU SCORE?

9 OR MORE: You are good at making connections: use your talents with the the Creativity Exercises. 6–8: You need to loosen up your thinking processes. LESS THAN 6: You are having trouble making new connections. The Creativity and Lateral Thinking cards can help you get into a more creative mind-set.

EMOTIONAL INTELLIGENCE

ANSWERS TO EQ-STYLE TEST
INVENTORY

Use the following key to work out your score for the Inventory.

SCORING

Q	a	b	Q	a	b	Q	a	b
1	0	1	6	0	1	11	0	1
2	0	1	7	1	0	12	0	1
3	0	1	8	0	1	13	1	0
4	1	0	9	1	0	14	0	1
5	0	1	10	0	1			

EMOTIONAL UNDERSTANDING TEST

1a: anger; b: happiness; c: fear; d: sadness. Score 1 point for each correct answer.
2: a: 1; b: 0; c: 3.

HOW DID YOU SCORE?

Add your score on the Emotional Understanding Test to your score from the Inventory.

18 AND ABOVE: You probably have high EI. You are good at understanding your own internal emotional processes and reading how other people feel, and can also use this knowledge to get on well with people and negotiate social situations successfully. A high EQ suggests that you might thrive in a career involving people management or personal contact (e.g., sales, human resources, caring profession, etc.). Don't take your abilities for granted, however—you need to keep them honed.

11–17: Your EI is probably within the average range. You do your best to be sensitive and empathetic, and keep your emotions in check where necessary, but it's not always easy. And while on the whole you try to get on with family, friends, and colleagues, you don't always manage your relationships to best effect.

10 OR LESS: You probably have low EI, and find it hard to understand other people or monitor and control your own emotions. This can make social situations a minefield, and relationships difficult. Even though you may be very good at your job, you might not achieve the workplace success you deserve because you're not managing colleagues, bosses, and underlings successfully. In general, the careers that best suit low EI people are solitary jobs or occupations that deal more with things and less with people (e.g., engineering, finance, IT). There's plenty of room for improvement.

LANGUAGE AND COMMUNICATION
SCORING FOR LANGUAGE AND COMMUNICATION TEST
LANGUAGE ABILITY STATUS TEST

1: Perfect, **3 points**; 1 or 2 mistakes, gets it right second time: **2 points**; 3 mistakes, stumbles second time: **1 point**.

2: Perfect, **3 points**; 1 mistake: **2 points**; 2 or 3 mistakes, **1 point**.

3: Perfect, **3 points**; 1 mistake: **2 points**; **2 or 3 mistakes: 1 point**.

4: 21 or more: **4 points**; 17–20: **3 points**; 13–16: **2 points**; 12 or less, **1 point**.

HOW DID YOU SCORE?

12–13: Your language skills are sharp. Keep them honed by trying the Challenges on the cards.

8–11: There are a few signs that your language abilities aren't up to scratch. You need to give yourself regular mental workouts—follow the advice in the chapter, and try the Challenges on the cards.

7 OR LESS: Your language skills show marked deficits. Try the test again at a time when you are less tired or stressed. If you get the same score, you may want to examine your diet, lifestyle, or health.

SPELLING TEST

1: unnecessary; 2: assassin; 3: government; 4: rhythm; 5: defendant; 6: (spelled correctly); 7: error; 8: ambassador; 9: indifference; 10: alienation; 11: receipt; 12: (spelled correctly); 13: parliament; 14: independent; 15: yacht; 16: sedimentary; 17: eliminate; 18: (spelled correctly); 19: doctrinaire; 20: deference; 21: fuchsia; 22: (spelled correctly); 23: tortoiseshell; 24: (spelled correctly)

HOW DID YOU SCORE?

Less than 10: Your spelling is bad, which can indicate poor linguistic ability. This may be linked to educational deficits or even dyslexia, but whatever the cause you can overcome it and learn to boost your linguistic abilities.

11–22: You can spell pretty well, but mistakes are creeping in. Some of these may be the result of lapses of memory for spelling rules, while others may be caused by poor linguistic ability. Combine memory and language exercises to make sure you don't make these mistakes in the future.

Full marks: Your spelling is of a high standard but do you know how to use all of those words properly? Practice the Exercises and boost your abilities still further.

ACKNOWLEDGMENTS

The author would like to thank the brilliant innovators whose many and varied contributions to improving our thinking skills inspired this work: S. Baron-Cohen, Edward de Bono, Philip Carter, D.Coleman, P. Howlin, L. Janda, N.J. Mackintosh, and G. Small.

FURTHER READING

De Bono, E., *Lateral Thinking*; Carter, P., *IQ and Psychometric Tests*; Janda, L., *The Psychologist's Book of Personality Tests*; Small, G., M.D., *The Memory Bible*.